The Collection
2020

compiled by John Field

EXPRESS NEWSPAPERS

hamlyn

An Hachette UK Company
www.hachette.co.uk

First published in Great Britain in 2019 by Hamlyn,
a division of Octopus Publishing Group Ltd, Carmelite House,
50 Victoria Embankment, London EC4Y 0DZ
www.octopusbooks.co.uk

Cartoons

British Cartoon Archive

Cartoons supplied by British Cartoon Archive
Cartoons compiled by John Field

PB ISBN 978 0 60063 477 5
HB ISBN 978 0 60063 646 5

A CIP catalogue record for this book is available from the British Library.

Printed and bound in China

10 9 8 7 6 5 4 3 2 1

Contents

See page 13

Introduction: Hidden Jokes

This year's collection features seven subsidiary characters from Giles's portfolio who sometimes appear in his cartoons but are not part of the main storyline being illustrated. They are not always immediately obvious to the reader, can easily appear to be just part of the cartoon's general background and sometimes even seem to be deliberately hidden from first sight. It seems clear that these characters are there as much to amuse the cartoonist himself as to contribute to the cartoon's humour.

The Parrot
The parrot joined the family in Christmas 1980 as a present from the children to Grandma (21 December 1980). It is obvious that Mother is not too happy about this addition to the already unruly and chaotic family. It is also clear from the start that the bird is not going to be a calming influence on them. Even at its first appearance, you can see trouble ahead. The cartoon shows the damage it has already inflicted on both the twins and, Young Ernie's earlier attempt to feed it has resulted in a bandaged finger.

Giles used the parrot over a period of almost ten years, with it appearing in a large number of cartoons and thirty of these are included here. It rarely appears without Grandma and it is obvious that she greatly enjoys its strongly independent character and its very disruptive impact on the family's life. Some of its favourite pastimes include pulling off the cloth of a fully laden table, bursting Christmas balloons, pulling out electrical leads and on one occasion even answering the telephone, much to Father's annoyance (10 January 1982).

Stinker (with camera)
This section features Stinker – the son of a neighbour. He seems to spend more time with the Giles family than with his own – maybe because he finds them more fascinating.

He is often seen getting up to all sorts of mischief but this collection concentrates on his obvious passion for observing and recording, on camera, many of the family's more unusual, and sometimes embarrassing, antics.

Rupert Bear
This section relates to another well-loved member of the *Express* Newspaper's group of cartoon characters. On the face of it, Rupert Bear was a friendly little chap with his checked trousers and his matching yellow scarf. It is surprising, therefore, that Giles always showed him in unpleasant situations, often hanging by his neck from a light fitting or door knob (27 November 1969) or being shot at by a posse of Giles family children (13 July 1971).

The possible explanation for this uncharacteristic behaviour on Giles's part was that he saw this other popular cartoon character as a strong rival to his family in readers' affections. Of course, this apparent animosity could simply have been Giles's sense of humour reacting to the innocence of this friendly little bear.

It should be noted, however, that a number of cartoons have been included in this section where, in fact, the bear being unfairly treated is not Rupert himself – they are, in fact, Teddy Bears –perhaps displaying a general antipathy by the cartoonist towards all toy bears.

Bewildered Baby George

Baby George (AKA George Jnr) suffers from being the only child of an over-anxious mother, Vera, who is usually shown as suffering from some ailment or being extremely stressed by national or other events, many of which do not affect her personally. The little features on his face portray a wide range of worries from total confusion or incomprehension about a situation he has found himself in, apprehension on what is about to happen, and various levels of surprise and fear on encountering many of the wonders of nature.

To make his plight even worse, it seems that the adult members of the family, including his mother, are completely unaware of the predicaments in which Baby George often finds himself. His mother is usually preoccupied with her own problems and even his grandmother and great grandmother (our cartoon Grandma) rarely notice his existence.

On only very rare occasions is he seen expressing pleasure or displaying any level of confidence. A glimmer of hope for his future is illustrated on 14 May 1974, where he is seems pleased at the thought of being auctioned off – perhaps to a better home, and on 6 April 1965 (in the section on Butch), where he is the only one of the children who finds the situation comforting.

Butch the Dog

The cartoon family dog, Butch is often involved in various catastrophes affecting the family home and this possibly reflected, on occasion, the real-life Butch's role in Giles's household at Hillbrow Farm. In Giles's cartoon world, Butch is often in hot water but can also be seen observing the family's activities with a mixture of dismay and surprise, and sometimes, amusement. He is also very good at hogging the fire during cold spells and slinking off when one of his misdemeanours is about to be uncovered.

See page 134

Butch seems to have a fairly loose relationship with the rest of the family but, on occasion, one senses a certain antipathy between him and Grandma (23 February 1986). Sometimes there is also a hint of dislike between him and Grandma's great love in the family – the parrot. This probably emanates from their original meeting, recorded in the first cartoon in this collection.

Frogs

From the mid 1960s, frogs suddenly arrive on the scene, again very much as incidental characters. There seems to be no explanation for their arrival. Presumably, Giles decided to increase his portfolio of sub-characters with the frogs in order to provide yet another humorous element into the general background of a cartoon. Usually the frogs appear singly but occasionally there are a number of them (14 March 1965) and sometimes they are toy frogs. On a number of occasions, they are used as yet another thing to upset poor little Baby George (22 June 1986) and, finally, could there be some sort of alliance between the frogs and Stinker (5 March 1972)?

Mice

As with the frogs, the introduction of mice seems to be mainly for Giles's own amusement as they never form part of the main storyline of any cartoon. Half of the twenty mice cartoons included here were produced during two relatively short periods – four between December 1965 and March 1966 and six between October and December 1966. It is possible that their arrival is a result of an infestation of these little creatures at Giles's farm or in one of its outbuildings. It is tempting to conclude that during these two periods, he was particularly conscious of their proliferation at home and this led to him including them as an extra element within his drawings (30 January 1972).

While all these characters are generally subservient to the main issue of each cartoon, Giles obviously felt compelled to include them in his work – probably as much for his own satisfaction as for that of his readers. They add greatly to my own enjoyment of Giles's cartoons and I hope that readers of this collection will find equal pleasure in spotting their miscellaneous appearances.

John Field

The Parrot

The parrot becomes a member of the Giles household. The significant impact it will have on the family's life is already apparent.

"You've bought Grandma a WHAT for Christmas?"

Sunday Express, 21 December 1980

Obviously Grandma and some of the children are delighted with the parrot's independent spirit, but Baby George is not so sure.

"'Soon as the shops open after Christmas back goes the damn parrot.'
'Not so,' says the parrot."

Sunday Express, 28 December 1980

12 The parrot discovers the sport of removing Grandma's glasses, which becomes an ongoing pastime. Newspapers were reporting a boom in weddings, possibly due to speculation about a marriage between Prince Charles and Lady Diana Spencer. Their engagement was announced two weeks later.

"That reminds me – you still owe me for the ring."

Daily Express, 10 February 1981

Three days earlier, Pope John Paul II made a call for more interfaith dialogue. The day before, the Spanish government's Congress of Deputies was taken over by members of the Guardia Civil in a coup, which failed when King Juan Carlos refused to co-operate. Presumably the parrot was expressing strong views on both subjects.

"If you wish to remain a permanent member of this family – no politics or religion!"

Daily Express, 24 February 1981

14 This was the night of the United Kingdom Census 1981 and, despite its name, Attila the Hun, the parrot turns out to be a female. I am not sure, anyway, that this newcomer to the family should be added for the purposes of the Census.

"Hold it, Dad! Attila the Hun's just laid another egg."

Sunday Express, 5 April 1981

"Fleet Street will give a bomb for this tape of what Dad said when Aunt Florrie phoned to say they were all coming to tea."

Sunday Express, 10 May 1981

It seems that the parrot objects to other birds on its property. The FA Cup Final that evening was a replay because the first Final, between Tottenham Hotspurs and Manchester City, played five days earlier, had ended in a 1–1 draw. Spurs won the replay 3–2.

"We can have our disco here tonight – there's nothing on TV except the Cup Final."

Daily Express, 14 May 1981

"How do you keep fireworks away from a pet who's just eaten all your Atomic Bangers?"

Daily Express, 5 November 1981

The parrot is fast becoming an authoritative member of the family but is not fully appreciated by everyone. It should be noted that this period contained some of the coldest, snowiest and severest winter weather ever recorded in the UK. The breaking pot shocks Baby George.

"No problem – he'll come out in the Land Rover and tow you home – only eight miles from here, you said?"

Sunday Express, 10 January 1982

On this occasion, the parrot appears to be helping its owner, Grandma. The cartoon is Giles's comment upon the Falklands Conflict which started two days earlier.

"But when the blast of war blows in our ears...Stiffen the sinews, Summon up the blood... Clear out the old air-raid shelter..."

Sunday Express, 4 April 1982

The parrot is helping the family's contribution to the war effort as well as adding to Baby George's almost permanent sense of bewilderment.

"Out come the old '39–'45 war jokes – 'If you want to help our boys you should send those socks to the enemy'."

Sunday Express, 25 April 1982

"Nothing in the post but the usual bills, oh, and a white feather from the lady you were discussing the Falkland war with."

Daily Express, 27 April 1982

The London Marathon took place on this day and the parrot has found another source of amusement.

"Call Dad and remind him he arranged last night to go on the Great Marathon Race this morning."

Sunday Express, 9 May 1982

"It's a summons from a burglar who broke in and stole half a bottle of Grandma's home-made wine and has never been the same since."

Sunday Express, 26 September 1982

The parrot seems oblivious to these new competitors for the family's airspace and Baby George is uncertain about things.

"Meet the latest member of the family – from today bats become a protected species."

Daily Express, 28 September 1982

The 32nd Miss World Pageant was held at the Royal Albert Hall in London on that day. Grandma does not seem too happy with changes to the pension system, matched by Baby George's consternation at the parrot's latest escapade.

"I'd skip the 'Good morning, Miss World'. She's just worked out what she's not going to get in the way of pensions."

Daily Express, 18 November 1982

E.T. the Extra-Terrestrial was the most popular film of 1982, but the family's activities were more concerned with Christmas. The parrot's contribution was obviously not welcomed by all, a feeling about to be added to by the family cat.

"Vera – If I've got any tears to shed this morning I give you my written guarantee right now they're not for E.T."

Daily Express, 9 December 1982

Grandma seems quite pleased with the parrot's resourceful approach to any food left lying around, or is it anticipation regarding the drink?

27

"My Happy New Year will begin when the decorations and the last mince pie are down and not before."

Sunday Express, 2 January 1983

28 The parrot is happy to steal food from even the most vulnerable member of the family – there was some doubt about the future of Aintree at this time but Young Ernie probably has a point. A slumbering Butch has not noticed that spider yet.

"What's the betting Aintree doesn't see a penny of it?"

Daily Express, 12 April 1983

The *Hitler Diaries* comprised sixty volumes and were supposedly written by Hitler himself, but were, in fact, forgeries written between 1981 and 1983. The parrot occasionally joins in with the children's games. What is Baby George swallowing?

"I didn't SAY she wrote them – I only said she COULD have written them."

Daily Express, 26 April 1983

30 The parrot is about to change the subject with one of its, by now, well-developed disruptive tricks. In her autobiography, *Out on a Limb*, American film star Shirley MacLaine referred to an affair with a British politician. Following some newspaper publicity about the man she stated that, simply, "an enterprising English journalist based in New York City... saw an opportunity to have some fun, and spiced up an otherwise dull [British] election". His article had reported that the man involved had "lost the tip of one finger".

"Vicar's got a tip off his little finger, does that mean he's having a wild affair with Shirley MacLaine?"

Daily Express, 5 June 1983

Another trick frequently enjoyed by the parrot. At the time, there was considerable concern about pornographic content in some videos and 1984 saw the introduction of state censorship within Britain through the British Board of Film Censors.

"That's the kind of video nasty I'd ban from the home – two reels of Grandma and Vera paddling in Benidorm."

Sunday Express, 13 November 1983

The parrot is taking advantage of a very hectic time in the family kitchen.

"I don't know who he is – he called and said 'I'm Father Christmas' and he's been here all afternoon."

Daily Express, 24 December 1983

Presumably the parrot wants that large piece of meat for itself.

"Hurry up, Mr Marathon – the other 20,141 left twenty minutes ago."

Sunday Express, 13 May 1984

Obviously Grandma approves of the parrot's attempts to annoy Butch the family's dog. The National Council for Voluntary Services had just produced a report about family happiness in the United Kingdom.

"This will put the NCVO report that Britain is a nation of Happy Families to the test
– here comes Uncle Sidney and his happy breed."

Sunday Express, 9 September 1984

"Noel! I've just won a Christmas holiday for one in the Bahamas – plane leave tonight!"

Daily Express, 20 December 1984

The parrot is causing disruption again. Baby George is not at all sure about spiders.

"Your electric fence didn't stop them coming to tea – they've all bought little rubber boots."

Sunday Express, 28 April 1985

"I only asked him to try his new uniform for school tomorrow and he suddenly remembered
he's got a recurrence of an old dormant ailment."

38 For once, the parrot is not the main antagonist. The TV refers to a forthcoming meeting between the two world leaders at Reykjavik, where the easing of tensions was discussed. For some reason Grandma strongly disapproves. Note the lock and chain on her handbag.

"Don't be so pessimistic, Grandma – not everything on TV ends with one of them standing the other one up at the altar."

Daily Express, 2 October 1986

The parrot is tempting fate in messing with Grandma. The Chess Grandmasters Association held six World Cup tournaments over 1988 and 1989, creating a wider interest in the game. At this time the fifth tournament was being held in Rotterdam.

"Why should I let him win as it's Father's Day? Check mate!"

Stinker (with camera)

Stinker, wishing to capture action, uses his friend Young Ernie, a captive actor for the time being. Davy Crockett was a 19th-century American frontiersman who was portrayed in a very popular film at this time entitled *Davy Crockett, King of the Wild Frontier*.

"I'm off duty in ten minutes, when I shall show Davy Crockett here who's King of the Wild Frontier."

Sunday Express, 20 May 1956

Stinker is recording this experiment with Baby George for posterity. Despite smoking during this period of illness, Churchill survived for another five years – thankfully we also know that, from later cartoons, Baby George suffered no long-term effects.

"Winston Churchill's doctor lets HIM smoke cigars while he's poorly."

Daily Express, 22 November 1960

Stinker is on the spot to record the police driver's misdemeanour. Presumably the patrol was intended to check the eyesight of private motorists, not the police drivers themselves,

"That's a handy start – you missed those NO ENTRY signs."

Daily Express, 19 July 1962

The US midterm elections took place the following November and were being held during the Vietnam War, which was causing a great deal of debate around the world. Despite losses, the Democrats, under Lyndon Johnson, retained control of Congress and the House of Representatives.

"Because you heard the lady say she supports President Johnson doesn't entitle you to go and hit her."

Sunday Express, 3 July 1966

The 1967 FA Cup Final took place two weeks later. It was the first to take place involving two teams from London and was called the "Cockney Cup Final". Baby George is not sure about those eyes.

"Stand by for action. Grandma's putting two and two together – the disappearance of her coupons and the arrival of your Cup Final tickets."

Sunday Express, 7 May 1967

Stinker obviously wishes to capture Chalkie's downfall for future use. The idea of having driving lessons for school children during holidays was being mooted in the US.

"I don't fancy your chances of survival if he comes round."

Daily Express, 6 July 1967

46 Stinker is there to record Father's failings. This relates to the first budget since the devaluation of the pound the previous November and increased taxes were expected. Baby George looks slightly vulnerable and Butch appears entranced by the patterns of smoke.

"Mum! Dad's 'If-they-tax-tobacco-again-I'm-definitely-giving-it-up' crisis is over."

Daily Express, 21 March 1968

Stinker focuses upon another of Baby George's discomforts, obviously organised by the twins.
Butch watches the event with interest and that bird appears to be feeding off Grandma's mop.

"And this comment from your music teacher – 'I hope your boy enjoys his holiday as much as I'm going to enjoy mine'..."

Sunday Express, 21 July 1968

48

Stinker cannot resist the opportunity to get this event on film while Vera's son, Baby George, has a more pressing problem on his mind. Prime Minister Harold Wilson had used the unfortunate Vera to describe a number of his colleagues, adding to her despair.

"Come now, it isn't as bad as all that. He didn't say you looked like them, he said they looked like you."

Daily Express, 6 May 1969

This relates to a film, with Alec Guinness as the lead, covering Hitler's final days in an underground bunker in Berlin. Most members of the family, including Baby George and Butch, have been given the Hitler treatment.

"She makes a better Hitler than Alec Guinness even without a moustache."

Sunday Express, 13 May 1973

Stinker was obviously hoping to get a "behind the scenes" exclusive.

"'Ere, YOU!"

Sunday Express, 27 May 1973

"Timber!"

Sunday Express, 22 December 1974

Stinker is prepared to risk all for his art while Baby George looks a little concerned, possibly about the stability of the structure.

"When I said build them a tree-house to keep them quiet, I didn't mean to include room service."

Sunday Express, 24 July 1977

Stinker has to use his telephoto zoom lens to get this long distance shot. Pedro's predecessor, Victor, fell to the ground one day and could not get up again – he died shortly afterwards. Interest in him was revived the next summer when his companion, Dribbles, gave birth to a female calf named Victoria. Dribbles has her eye on the newcomer.

"Grandma doesn't mind them naming churches and cathedrals after her, but I don't think she'll go a lot on sex-mad giraffes."

Daily Express, 22 October 1977

Even Stinker is voting for the turkey's reprieve but it is obvious that Grandma and Butch are, for once, in agreement in disapproving of the verdict.

"Right – on the show of hands Sebastian gets a reprieve – one of you go to the shop and get six large tins of corned beef."

Sunday Express, 17 December 1978

Hang-gliding had become a popular sport. Young Ernie is not accepting blame and Baby George is the only one showing any real concern – in fact, Butch is thoroughly enjoying Grandma's situation. For Stinker, it is simply another Giles family incident to record.

"Can you imagine what she'd have said if I'd said no she couldn't have a go at my hang-glider?"

Daily Express, 28 December 1978

A period of food shortages with Grandma prepared to do her best for the family. Baby George is more concerned about his toy soldier marching out of his grasp and Stinker has turned his professional attention towards the fairer sex.

"Fifteen rounds for who's having my last pound of rump."

Daily Express, 25 May 1979

The country was experiencing an oil crisis at this time and Stinker is recording the Father's dishonesty – possibly for future negotiating advantage in collusion with young Ernie.

"I don't think Dad's eight miles to work by bike is saving as much petrol as Mum thinks."

Daily Express, 28 June 1979

Stinker again records a Giles family event while, for a change, the giant fake spider is used to shock Vera instead of Baby George.

"I don't think Auntie Esther meant her present to be worn OVER your topcoat, Dad."

Daily Express, 27 December 1979

"I don't think she got the job, Dad"

Sunday Express, 3 February 1980

Stinker could not resist the temptation to expand his portfolio. Prince Philip had taken up painting and received a mixed reception.

"Sotheby's said Prince Philip's painting would benefit from a course in life studies."

Sunday Express, 15 November 1981

Stinker is capturing the family's new "environmentally friendly" lawn maintenance acquisition
with Baby George again showing consternation about a spider.

"Mind the new lawnmower – Dad couldn't decide between a ride on air-cushioned or cylinder type."

Sunday Express, 28 March 1982

62 Stinker is again expanding his portfolio, but probably for a different category from that two cartoons earlier. The 1987 General Election took place a few days later and was the third consecutive election victory for the Conservative Party under Margaret Thatcher.

"Never mind who I'm voting for – which of them let you in here?"

Father has obviously expressed his displeasure too strongly for the young ears of Baby George and the twins. Tennis player McEnroe was known to swear on court when under pressure and Prince Charles had been similarly accused on occasions.

"Dad's been listening to too much McEnroe and Prince Charles."

Sunday Express, 2 July 1989

Rupert Bear and Teddy Bears

The United Nations General Assembly In New York had attracted an unprecedented number of world leaders and China was increasingly seen as a threat. The general atmosphere in the room is tense, with the Teddy Bear enjoying his last cigarette in front of a firing squad and Baby George and his mother shocked by Grandma's scary comment.

"With all UNO playing about in New York it's a fine opportunity for Red China to take over the world."

Daily Express, 21 September 1960

The severe winter weather had cancelled many football matches and Father has found an effective way of achieving peace and quiet while responsible for the children. Baby George is probably unsure about this situation and the Teddy Bear doesn't care anymore.

"I told him as there's no football he can stay at home and amuse the children."

Sunday Express, 20 January 1963

The Teddy Bear is being used for target practice at a time when the world seemed to be an increasingly dangerous place. Baby George is being introduced to the concept of very loud noises.

"Nothing brings on Vera's hiccups quicker than the Americans dropping bombs in the interest of world peace."

Sunday Express, 9 August 1964

Rupert seems to be hanging free while the other toys are more secure on the top shelf of the shop.
The shop cat is not sure about the little girl's mouse.

"That one makes me nervous. If she's still paying me full price for her cigarettes she must be having me on something else."

Daily Express, 17 January 1967

This is another example of Rupert hanging around. Baby George is wary of his mother's swarm of germs while Young Ernie tries to help.

"Pity. Vera's thrived on it all her life."

Daily Express, 27 November 1969

Four days later, the postal workers went back to work after seven weeks on strike. At least Rupert has one friend in the family – a concerned Baby George is trying to protect him after a vicious attack on the little bear's legs.

"Boy! I'm glad I'm not editor of the 'Dear Sir' column when the post strike ends."

Daily Express, 4 March 1971

The family's antagonism towards bears is obviously not limited to Rupert.

"What a pity. It'll mean your cousin Henrietta won't be able to bring back any more little souvenir Spanish bulls."

Daily Express, 6 May 1971

This time it is the twins who are being nasty to Rupert while one of the family's "lovable" pets has stolen from Baby George and Butch has again shown his dislike of postmen.

"While you're writing to the *Express* about 'You and your lovable pet'..."

Daily Express, 13 July 1971

Both Rupert and Baby George, among others, are badly shocked by the attempt to bring down the house while Butch sleeps through the whole thing.

"It's their new game – they read about the woman who slammed her door and the house fell down."

Daily Express, 23 January 1975

In addition to the Teddy Bear being bound up, this cartoon shows a dismayed Baby George being persecuted by a young playful Butch and that large spider again. Stinker is attempting to get an unusual photo of Grandma, no doubt to support Young Ernie's claim.

"Natural History Museum? We have photographic proof of another monster
– colour mostly black, fur round neck, powerful flippers..."

Daily Express, 24 November 1975

A Teddy Bear is again being treated unkindly, this time by Stinker. Butch has finished off whatever Grandma was drinking.

"According to Grandma, she worked hard all her life; brought up 14 children on 10 shillings a week; did 12 hours a day down a mine; got a Karate Black Belt; and she's very happy."

Daily Express, 23 September 1977

Even Donald Duck does not like Rupert – maybe there was a disagreement over the pretty doll. Stinker has his camera ready to capture Father's release. Butch is bewildered by the whole situation and Baby George has been imprisoned, perhaps for his own safety.

"Dad, Mum says would you like a mince pie while we're waiting for the fire brigade?"

Daily Express, 24 December 1979

That year, Gabriella Brum of Germany won the Miss World Pageant in London. The following day, she resigned because her boyfriend objected to her future obligations as Miss World, adding that she did not want to be "flying through the world... for a year". Rupert does not look too comfortable in the air either.

"I know the feeling, mate."

Daily Express, 13 November 1980

This cartoon appeared in the middle of the Falklands Conflict where Harrier Jump Jets performed a major role flying from the aircraft carriers *HMS Invincible* and *HMS Hermes*. Rupert is likely to go flying any minute.

"Unconfirmed report that one of your jump jets has made a direct hit on Dad's cornflakes."

Daily Express, 4 May 1982

Rupert does not appear to be very much at ease and Baby George doesn't look any happier. *The Good Life* was a very popular TV programme where a young couple try to live as simply as possible.

"Remember last night? 1983 is going to be different – we're all going to live like they do in *The Good Life* on TV."

Daily Express, 04 January 1983

Rupert is again being used as a target, this time by Stinker. This cartoon appeared during the British Open Snooker Championship being held in Sheffield. The Canadian player, Kirk Stevens, was accused by another player of being "as high as a kite" while playing. Shortly afterwards, Stevens admitted to an addiction to cocaine.

"She's won me moneybox, piggy bank, half an Easter egg, me conkers and me knife – I reckon she's on dope!"

Daily Express, 11 April 1985

Bewildered Baby George

Baby George is taken aback by this strange creature. Two days earlier, the glamorous American film star, Marilyn Monroe, married Arthur Miller, a serious and intellectual writer. Unfortunately, they divorced five years later.

"Witness Egghead playing the Intellectual-to-marry-Marilyn Monroe technique."

Sunday Express, 1 July 1956

The cat may catch the bird before *it* catches the creepy crawly before *it* completely freaks out Baby George.

81

"If Grandma's bought a short dress I'm going to leave home."

Daily Express, 31 January 1958

Baby George is amazed by the strength of that ant while the children are concerned about their father's plans for their future.

"Assuming their teachers do go on strike and we've got to have them at home a few more weeks..."

Sunday Express, 9 April 1961

Baby George, about to lose his milk bottle, discovers that the beach has some very worrying wildlife. The crab's friend has just ruined the twins' day at the seaside. Young Ernie is concerned about increasing tension between the USSR and the Western powers.

"Ask ourselves – what are we, as responsible citizens, doing to ease the tension in Berlin?"

Sunday Express, 26 August 1962

A bewildered Baby George has just realized that Grandma's log is alive, his mother has found a comfortable seat and Stinker is about to add a young alligator to his animal collection.

"It says here, Vera, that story about live alligators in the canal has been denied."

Daily Express, 30 April 1963

Grandma does not seem to be responding positively to all this attention while, between them,
Bridget and the kitten have tied up Baby George in knots.

"The lengths some people will go in the hope of a cut if Grandma gets her pension raised."

Sunday Express, 8 November 1964

It looks as if an innocent Baby George is about to come to grips with a large wasp. Young Ernie, seeing trouble ahead, is making use of an opportunity provided by America's Gemini 9A spaceflight passing overhead.

"Dad – I think a piece of Gemini 9A is just going to land on Mr. Jones's greenhouse."

Sunday Express, 5 June 1966

Baby George seems attracted by that wasp again. At this time, there was considerable trouble developing between Alexander Dubček, First Secretary of the Communist Party of Czechoslovakia, and the USSR, which led to an invasion of the country by Soviet troops later that month.

"I've put hundreds of 'em in Grandma's Guinness and they don't do her any harm."

Daily Express, 1 August 1968

Baby George is amazed by this latest scientific discovery. At this time, the financial situation was considered to be the most serious since the Great Depression of the 1920s. Within the family, Grandma had a certain well-earned reputation.

"She'll be lucky. Because of the grave international monetary crisis I took the precaution of removing the contents of me piggy bank this time."

Sunday Express, 8 December 1968

The twins often make the most of Baby George as a source of entertainment, much to his dismay.
The European fashion houses had decreed that the days of the mini were over.

"That puts Grandma bang on target."

Daily Express, 27 January 1970

Baby George is not sure about the attention he is getting from Butch and the frog looks glum.

"I think you're as safe kissing Butch as you know who."

Daily Express, 17 September 1970

Something seems to be upsetting Baby George.
Two weeks earlier, the Bank of England had produced new £5 notes – this cartoon suggests
that there was a problem at the time with counterfeit copies.

"I'll tell you why we're suspicious – because this is the fifth fiver you've changed this morning for a penny oxo cube"

Sunday Express, 28 November 1971

This time it is an annoyed-looking duck that is upsetting Baby George.
As the newspaper's headlines show, the world was full of bad news.

"I suppose the news could be worse – we could have Georgie Best moving in to live with us."

Sunday Express, 23 July 1972

Baby George is, again, not totally comfortable with the situation and Butch may not be able
to continue his slumbers for much longer.

"We packed the chilldren off to the Safari Park for a bit of peace."

Sunday Express, 25 March 1973

For once, Baby George seems pleased – perhaps at the prospect of finding a new, less worrying home. Butch is slowly catching on to the situation.

"Putting children up for adoption on TV has started something."

Obviously a new family Christmas present – Baby George has some doubts about the whole thing but, of course, Grandma has entered into the spirit of things a little too enthusiastically.

"Mum! Grandma's gone down behind the piano."

Daily Express, 28 December 1974

Baby George is not sure what is happening and Young Ernie is in real trouble.
This was a period of high building costs nationally.

"Mum, you know the new extension Dad's building himself to save massive builder's bills?"

Sunday Express, 2 March 1975

A sunburned Baby George is horrified by this latest revelation about nature's wide range of creepy-crawlies, while his mother, Vera, is equally horrified by the actions of that crab.

"That's how the Aussies do it – bowl 'em on the feet, make 'em hop out of their crease, and BINGO!!"

Daily Express, 13 June 1975

Yet another unpleasant surprise for Baby George.

"I've written and told the *Express* the only way they can solve my Christmas present problem is by sending me a cheque."

Daily Express, 4 December 1975

Baby George is uncertain about how to respond to this show of friendship from the frog, while Butch seems to be ill-treating Father Christmas. I suspect Father has had enough of the festive season.

"I'm having a Bank-Holiday party – bring Harry, Georgie, Dickie, Punghi, Ronnie, Wilmer and the gang and ask Buggsie to bring his drums and Hi Fi with him."

Sunday Express, 2 January 1977

Another uncomfortable surprise for Baby George. Jimmy Young was an American heavyweight boxer who beat George Foreman at this time. He was renowned for his awkward, defensive style and counterpunching. Maybe Giles felt that these attributes would be useful at a time when relations between Washington and Moscow were very tense.

"Here's a story to warm the cockles of your heart, Vera – it will take at least two million years to erode the astronauts' footprints on the moon."

Daily Express, 16 May 1977

A wide range of insects seem to be fascinated by Baby George, much to his dismay. The children kept this promise for three years until the infamous parrot joined the family in Christmas 1980 (see 21 December 1980).
Butch will never catch Natalie.

"Repeat again, everybody: 'Mother does not want any new puppies, budgies, pussies, or bunnies for Christmas'."

Daily Express, 16 December 1977

Baby George is not too happy about this perilous situation – those hands probably belong to Stinker.
Grandma looks as if her horse has lost again and Young Ernie's observation is not very popular
with all members of the family.

"If you get forty lashes for one small drink like they're going to give 'em in Egypt,
you botty would be tingling, Uncle Charlie."

Sunday Express, 12 February 1978

That spider is way above Baby George's head but he has experienced similar situations before and they never ended well. That year, there were 25 days of non-stop World Cup football on TV finishing on 25 June and, on the 26th, Wimbledon fortnight started on TV.

"Let there be no moaning at the bar when our Wimbledon fortnight comes round."

Daily Express, 9 June 1978

Baby George meets a new horror and Butch is about to add to Vera's woes.

"Vera thinks she's helping the BBC save its £130 million by not switching it on."

Sunday Express, 2 March 1980

Baby George is troubled by another spider. Stinker is up to his tricks again and the parrot is about to cause more mayhem.

"Rejoice good Christian men – the group's arrived."

Daily Express, 24 December 1981

Baby George is shocked by the fate of the Jack in a Box and the parrot is about to cause another upset.
Is it possible that it is working in league with Young Ernie under the table? Grandma is commenting on
a debate at the time about re-introducing hanging.

"Here come three of my good reasons for bringing back hanging."

Sunday Express, 21 March 1982

Baby George is again tormented by a giant spider, thanks to Stinker, while his mother, Vera, dozes alongside him. However, the parrot is about to wake everyone up by bursting a large balloon.

"Hoots everybody! Grandma and her sister are back from their Over Sixties Hogmanay party."

Daily Express, 31 December 1984

Butch the Dog

With a gloomy forecast relating to the Budget, Butch has chosen a bad morning to misbehave. Baby George appears to be unusually happy considering the circumstances – unlike the remainder of the family. That roller skate may not help the situation.

"Look on it as a sort of 'protective custody' until he's gone to work."

Daily Express, 6 April 1965

Butch's thieving action obviously upset the basket, which has caused considerable anxiety for Baby George. This cartoon followed a period of beef shortage across the country.

"As we haven't had beef for so long I thought I'd be rash and treat ourselves to a piece of sirloin."

Sunday Express, 12 May 1974

A young Butch is developing his skills in upsetting Baby George as well as picking up on the family's general antipathy towards bears.

"Here we are, Einstein – a field in which you cannot fail to shine."

Daily Express, 15 July 1975

"I try my hardest to like the Labour Government and then they do things like this…"

Daily Express, 8 April 1976

Butch knows that he is in trouble again, even though he is not really responsible. Graham Sutherland painted Churchill's portrait in 1954. Churchill hated it and it was never put on display. After Lady Churchill's death in 1977, it became clear that the painting had been destroyed some months after it was delivered to the sitter.

"We're not destroying a great work of art – we're preserving it with a coat of creosote."

Sunday Express, 15 January 1978

The twins are finding new uses for pastry and Butch is not sure what is happening. Baby George is also confused. At this time Parliament was discussing the re-introduction of hanging but it was eventually rejected.

"No, we can not hang Auntie Bertha because she wants to bring back hanging."

Daily Express, 19 July 1979

This summer, the good weather was spoiled by huge swarms of greenflies. Butch, however, is not allowing it to deter him from his unwise interest in wasps.

"Dad – Grandma's just swallowed six thousand eight hundred and seventy-three greenflies."

Sunday Express, 29 July 1979

Butch is developing his inherent hunting skills by starting with an easy prey.

115

"Just two more days of the Year of the Child then the Year of the Adult takes over in this house."

Sunday Express, 30 December 1979

Butch has found an Easter chick and Baby George is taken by surprise.

"Finish making Grandma's Easter egg later and tell her breakfast is ready."

Sunday Express, 6 April 1980

As a hunting breed, Airedales are renowned for their courage and strength but here Butch, a town dog, is being seen off by rather a small rabbit.

"Here we go again – every time BP sticks the price up, it's: 'Carol! Have you seen the pony?'"

Daily Express, 11 June 1981

Butch knows that there is going to be trouble – increases in petrol prices had been announced.

"Dad! You've won a smashing family speed boat – can I tell Mum?"

Sunday Express, 17 January 1982

Butch is about to get into trouble again and Baby George is unsure about that biscuit. The parrot is taking an interest in the proceedings. Ray Buckton was General Secretary of ASLEF, the rail drivers' trade union, and Sir Peter Parker was Chairman of the British Railways Board.

"The Valentines Grandma sent to Ray Buckton and Sir Peter Parker – they're charging her for sending obscene literature through the post."

Sunday Express, 14 February 1982

The "Festival of India" was a six-month celebration of Indian culture and art held in Britain during 1982.
Butch is not too impressed by one aspect of Indian musical culture.

"Tell your little friend Singh to take them back to the Indian Festival right now!"

Daily Express, 23 March 1982

Butch is again heading for trouble and Baby George is being plagued by that spider once more.
There was considerable concern about the violent content of a number of films distributed
on video cassette, which resulted in a large number of videos being banned.

"How do you get in touch with the people who banned those video horror films?"

Daily Express, 2 September 1982

Butch senses that there is trouble ahead. This was in the run-up to the long-running miners' strike the following year and Young Ernie is probably voicing Giles's thoughts on the subject.

"That was very rude to tell Aunty that a couple of weeks at the coalface would make her think differently about the miners' strike."

Sunday Express, 6 March 1983

The 1983 General Election was three weeks later. Yuri Andropov was the General Secretary of the Soviet Union Communist Party and Screaming Lord Sutch was Leader of the Official Monster Raving Loony Party. Butch, unwisely, is more interested in the wasp.

"Dad this is Vince – he's torn between Mrs. Thatcher, Andropov and Screaming Lord Sutch."

Sunday Express, 15 May 1983

Butch's indiscretion is being captured on film by Stinker.

"Butch must learn that the law that says it's all right for pretty nude dancers to bite policemen, doesn't apply to grumpy Airedales."

Sunday Express, 6 November 1983

Butch is keeping up his campaign against Grandma. That February was the coldest month in the UK for many years whereas, at the same time, British TV was showing the Indian cricket team playing against Australia in Melbourne in a one-day series, under a very strong sun.

"My heart bleeds for our poor cricketers losing out there in all that terrible sun."

Sunday Express, 23 February 1986

Butch has his mind on other things.

"Trust her to win both bets – right about Bob Geldof and right about Bobby Robson."

Daily Express, 12 June 1986

Butch is making sure that he benefits from Grandma's windfall. The room, unfortunately, is likely to get much cooler when that log breaks the French window.

"Grandma's making sure she gets her extra £5 worth."

Sunday Express, 18 January 1987

Frogs

The frogs are escaping Father's anger but Baby George's teddy bear is not so lucky,
much to the child's unhappiness.

"Those tenants who've only got snakes in their bathroom are lucky."

Sunday Express, 14 March 1965

Stinker has brought the wasp into the classroom – the books and waste paper bin traps are also, no doubt, his work and, almost certainly, he is responsible for that frog. The teacher may find it difficult to love his lively mind by the time she reaches her desk.

As somebody said about the teachers' conference: "Teachers are not factory foremen. They should be men and women who love children and their lively minds."

Daily Express, 14 April 1966

Stinker has discovered a new use for the frog and Baby George has found something else to be worried about.
That clockwork mouse appears again.

"They're signing a two-day truce with Grandma. They won't play any Christmas jokes on her if she promises she won't sing."

Daily Express, 24 December 1968

I think this present did, in fact, go back to the shop, whereas the parrot, another of the children's troublesome Christmas presents for Grandma nine years later, became a permanent member of the household. Stinker records the monkey's fleeting stay.

"You say you've bought it for Grandma for Christmas and I say it's going back to the shop first thing in the morning."

Sunday Express, 5 December 1971

This is one of the occasions when the frog and the mouse appear together, possibly due to Stinker.
Stoke City beat Chelsea 2–1 in the League Cup.

"I'm not so concerned about this Daniel getting out of the lion's den
as I am about Chelsea and Stoke kicking off on TV."

Sunday Express, 5 March 1972

"Wake up dear, 'tis Father's Day. Joint presentation – one jar of tadpoles."

Sunday Express, 16 June 1974

The Religious Education Council works to strengthen such provision in schools in England and Wales but it probably did not have this in mind. Stinker has really entered into the spirit of the subject being taught and may have been involved in Mr Wilmot's fate.

"I shouldn't put that one in, Sir – that's Mr. Wilmot, the maths master."

Daily Express, 28 October 1977

The frog seems to have become part of the furniture. Two seasons later the football programme moved back again to Saturday evenings so the golfers' change of habits was relatively short-lived.

"One thing about moving 'Match of the Day' to Sunday – it gets 'em home earlier for lunch."

Sunday Express, 7 September 1980

The frog looks upset, probably wondering what happened to the water.

"Daddy, the man next door's syphoning your bath water to clean his car."

Daily Express, 27 January 1983

"Don't forget you're picking up Auntie Pauline and Uncle Jim for lunch."

Sunday Express, 29 April 1984

Father's day of peace and the egret's hopes are lost.

"There you are! You didn't think we would let you spend Father's Day on your own."

Sunday Express, 16 June 1985

Baby George is again shocked by the natural world and its wonders. England's football match was in Mexico, against Argentina, in which Maradona scored his infamous "Hand of God" goal. Stinker has his camera with him so it is possible that he caught the incident on film.

"What do you mean – 'On your feet, everyone or we'll be late for the game!'?
We arranged this picnic before we even knew they'd be playing."

Sunday Express, 22 June 1986

Mice

No doubt the mouse is not sorry to see them go back to school.

"Of course I'm sorry you've all got to go back to boarding school – your mother's sorry you've got to go back to school – I bet your teacher's sorry you've got to go back to school."

Sunday Express, 2 September 1962

"Grandma, if you can't take your ice skates off stop stamping your feet to get warm."

Sunday Express, 27 January 1963

The 118th Grand National was run at Aintree six days after this cartoon appeared and there were considerable worries about horse doping at this time. The mouse seems to be more interested in the conversation taking place between the dogs.

"How about one of you tasting his food for dope for a change?"

Sunday Express, 15 March 1964

Goldie the Golden Eagle had escaped from London Zoo and, after four days on the run, was captured the day after this cartoon appeared. The mouse hopefully makes it to the fence.

143

"That's all I hear – 'How come you never take a run out and get your pictures in the papers?'"

Sunday Express, 19 December 1965

It is to be hoped that, in that household, the mouse and the cat are friends.

Following yesterday's story of a man who thought it "diabolical" that he should not be allowed to gum up
all other traffic while he exercised his doggy in comfort...

Daily Express, 13 January 1966

A few days earlier, the Soviet space probe, Venera 3, landed on the surface of Venus and scientists discovered more about the "Doppler Shift" phenomenon. Stinker's note is, perhaps, a reference to the subject as is the experiment with the trajectory of the apple but the releasing of the three blind mice is a mystery.

"Now, instruments monitoring the space probe's radio transmissions indicated a 'Doppler Shift'
which is tantamount to a change in the wavelength, or frequency, of a series of soundwaves caused
by the movement between Luna and Jodrell Bank."

Daily Express, 8 February 1966

That mouse is taking advantage of the domestic conversation taking place.

"I know what you're thinking – you're thinking you wish someone would run off with ME
and dump me outside Manchester University."

Sunday Express, 20 February 1966

The mouse looks comfortable. Baby George is getting all tied up, much to *his* discomfort. One month later, Prime Minister Harold Wilson called a snap election because he had only a small majority of just four MPs. His Government was returned with a majority of 96 seats.

"It's too bad of Mr. Wilson to keep us all in this state of nervous tension about the election date."

Sunday Express, 27 February 1966

Four days earlier, the Pope and the Archbishop of Canterbury, met to exchange fraternal greetings. They hoped for a new atmosphere of Christian fellowship between the Roman Catholic and the Anglican Churches.
The vicar is anticipating problems following this development – even the mouse has acquired ammunition.

"Most verily I say unto thee: 'Hop it'."

Sunday Express, 27 March 1966

This is not the only time that Grandma has been accused of stealing produce from that allotment holder for the Harvest Festival – the mouse, in turn, is also helping itself.

"You didn't plough any fields and scatter – you nicked that marrow from my allotment on the way here."

Sunday Express, 2 October 1966

Baby George is unhappy – £500 sounds a lot of money to him. A new Act in 1966 proposed that if workers went on strike to enforce immediate payment of any award, they would be liable to a fine of £500. Maybe the mouse is feeding the cat as an act of self-preservation.

"That's his best yet. If he grants our claim for extra pocket money we will be liable to a fine of £500."

Sunday Express, 16 October 1966

Hopefully the mouse will live to see another day. The Miss World Pageant was held at the Lyceum Ballroom in London four days later and was won by Reita Faria of India, the first Asian delegate to win the Miss World title.

"Come in, Fred – the wife's entertaining a few Miss World candidates for tea."

Sunday Express, 13 November 1966

With a bit of luck, the mice will fall onto that bale of straw. The British Government's Economic Sanctions were expected to bring down the minority Rhodesian Government in a matter of weeks but it was later considered that they had had limited success.

"How the hell is you laying off your food in protest against sanctions going to help your sister in Rhodesia, tell me that?"

Sunday Express, 18 December 1966

The children are emphasizing an important point promoted by the Council at that time –
even normally silent Baby George is joining in – in his own special way.
Obviously the mouse also finds the noise ear-splitting.

"It is the easiest thing in the world for a child to detect that you're not really listening to him."
...Marriage Guidance Council. Especially if they can see your ear-plugs.

Daily Express, 20 June 1969

That bone must have been left over from one of Grandma's late-night feasts. Baby George is confused again. This is towards the end of the Hong Kong Influenza Pandemic which had started the previous year.

"Don't fly off the handle, Grandma – we're only using your bed while our Christmas present's got flu."

Daily Express, 30 December 1969

"Can't come out today, boys – thanks to that fool of an M.P. calling women 'inferior and second-class citizens'."

Sunday Express, 30 January 1972

156   The mice are obviously unafraid of a very drowsy Butch. Baby George is taken aback by an unexpected smell
and probably the subject matter being discussed, and it looks as if the clockwork frog is about to jump.

"Now you and me are going to have a little chat about the facts of life.
Lesson One: We're all going to stop calling me 'Duckie'."

Daily Express, 18 April 1974

The Daily Star was launched from Manchester on this day and was originally available only in the North and the Midlands. The mouse must feel safe with all attention being focused upon Grandma's occupation of the toilet and the twins are passing the time by juggling with a disorientated Baby George.

"Grandma! That's enough Ooh! Cor! Wow! and Well I never! We'd ALL like to have a look at the new *Daily Star*."

Daily Express, 2 November 1978

It seems Natalie the cat does not mind sharing her milk with the mouse and Butch looks on in amazement. Ayatollah Khomeini had returned to Iran and become its Supreme Leader. It was reported that he then reneged upon an agreement made with the U.S. President, Jimmy Carter. Grandma's sentiments are obviously with the Ayatollah.

"And if I had the price of the fare I'd fly over and belt her one."

Sunday Express, 2 December 1979

The clockwork mouse has drawn Natalie the cat's attention away from the two live ones nearby.
The parrot is up to his normal tricks with a balloon and Butch is hiding from it all.

"It's the plumber we ordered in August – he can come and do the drain this afternoon."

Daily Express, 24 December 1982

All the cartoons in this book were copied from material in Carl Giles' own private archive, a huge collection of artwork, ephemera and correspondence, which is held by the British Cartoon Archive at the University of Kent. Carl Giles had been cartoonist for Lord Beaverbrook's *Daily* and *Sunday Express* for almost 20 years, when on 20 March 1962 the Conservative M.P. Sir Martin Lindsay tabled a motion deploring "the conduct of Lord Beaverbrook in authorizing over the last few years in the newspapers controlled by him more than 70 adverse comments on members of the royal family who have no means of replying".

Lindsay was wrong about the royal family having no means of reply. That day Prince Philip also vented his anger at Beaverbrook's campaign, during a press reception at the British Embassy in Rio de Janeiro. According to the paper's Brazil representative, the Prince declared that, "The *Daily Express* is a bloody awful newspaper. It is full of lies, scandal and imagination. It is a vicious paper."

When the *Daily Express* reported this the next day, Giles decided to treat it as a joke. He knew the royal family enjoyed his cartoons; they often asked for the artwork. This had begun in 1948, when Prince Philip was sent a cartoon on the State Opening of Parliament, and over the next few years Giles received a steady stream of requests from Buckingham Palace for original drawings.

Left: *Two of Giles's recurring hidden characters, Stinker and Bewildered Baby George, had rare leading roles on 22 November 1960.*

Giles drew the diminutive Lord Beaverbrook being escorted through the Traitor's Gate at the Tower of London, with a headsman's axe and block standing ready in the background. The caption repeated Prince Philip's condemnation of the *Daily Express*, but added laconically: "'Ah well,' said Lord B., as they trotted him off to the Tower, 'at least he takes it or he wouldn't know it was a bloody awful newspaper.'"

This was a brilliant response, which did much to defuse the situation. When Giles's cartoon was printed the next day, *Daily Express* staff were surprised to receive a phone call from the Queen's press secretary, with a message for Giles that "Her Majesty requests today's cartoon to commemorate one of her husband's most glorious indiscretions."

Giles sent off the artwork and in May 1962 found himself invited to "a small informal luncheon party" at Buckingham Palace with the Queen and Prince Philip. "I was filled with absolute dread," Giles recalled afterwards. "But as soon as she started to talk I was put at my ease…There were about half a dozen corgis running about in a completely uncontrolled state. Suddenly the Queen shouted, 'HEP'. It was like a bark from a sergeant major. The corgis immediately stood to attention. Then filed out of the room."

After the lunch Giles mischievously drew a cartoon of the guests leaving with corgi-savaged trousers. He sent it to the Queen, who returned her thanks through one of her private secretaries, noting that she was "glad that you got away without having lost, at least to the best of her knowledge, so much as a shred of your trousers".

After that Giles became what one *Daily Express* journalist called "a kind of cartooning jester to the royal family". By the time he retired in 1991 the royal family had more than 40 of his original drawings, the largest number being owned by Prince Philip, who shared Giles's anarchic view of the world.

The British Cartoon Archive, based at the University of Kent's Templeman Library in Canterbury, is dedicated to the history of British cartooning over the last two hundred years. It holds the artwork for more than 150,000 British political and social-comment cartoons, plus large collections of comic strips, newspaper cuttings, books and magazines. Its website at www.cartoons.ac.uk has over 200,000 cartoon images, including the majority of Carl Giles's published work.